Dream

of the

Gone-From City

T0079889

Dream

of the

Gone-From City

Barbara Edelman

Carnegie Mellon University Press
Pittsburgh 2017

Acknowledgments

Grateful acknowledgment is made to the editors of the following publications in which these poems first appeared:

5 AM: "What She Taught Me," "The Modulations of My Mother's Body"; *Askew*: "Adirondacks, May," "This cold night will turn us"; *Blue Mesa Review*: "Shopping at Ross Dress for Less"; *Central Park*: "The Pedal-Duck Toy"; *Cimarron Review*: "Geometry Problem"; *La Fovea*: "Bordeaux"; *Pittsburgh City Paper*: "Something Is Digging"; *Pittsburgh Poetry Review*: "Cat Act," "The Carriage House"; *Pittsburgh Post-Gazette*: "Cardinal Flight"; *Pittsburgh Quarterly*: "For Patti"; *Poet Lore*: "Dead Languages"; *Prairie Schooner*: "Blizzard"; *Raleigh Review*: "It is nor hand nor foot in mouth"; *Southern Indiana Review*: "Cloud Father"(as "Dream Father/Cloud Father"); *Zox Populi* (digital): "The River"; *Zone Three*: "The Writing of Desire"

"Maple Grove" appeared in *World to Come*: *Anthology of Finalists for the 2015 Raynes Poetry Prize*. Blue Thread Books and Music, 2015.

"Dream of the Gone-From City" appeared in *Along These Rivers: Poetry and Photography from Pittsburgh*. Poets for Humanity, 2008.

"Adirondacks, May" appeared in the anthology *Encore: More of Parallel Press Poets*. Parallel Press, 2006.

"Geometry Problem" was published in *A Fine Excess: Contemporary Literature at Play*. Sarabande Books, 2001.

Several of the poems in this collection were published in the chapbooks *Exposure* (Finishing Line Press, 2014) and *A Girl in Water* (Parallel Press, 2002).

Grateful thanks to Gerald Costanzo and the staff of Carnegie Mellon University Press.

Thanks to the writers/friends/teachers who have provided support and feedback on poems: Liz Ahl, Marilyn Annucci, Dorothy Barresi, Melissa Bender, Jim Bogen, Toi Derricotte, Gwen Ebert, Lynn Emanuel, Pam Goldman, Yona Harvey, Joy Katz, Chuck Kinder, Nancy Koerbel, Sharon McDermott, Ellen McGrath Smith, Sandra Mitchell, Jeff Oaks, Ed Ochester, John Schulman and Judy Vollmer.

Thanks to the Pennsylvania Council on the Arts for an individual artist grant in poetry and to the Vermont Studio Center and Virginia Center for the Creative Arts for residency fellowships.

Thanks to my wonderful extended family for their encouragement and support.

Book design by Connie Amoroso

to Dorothy—with thanks

and to the memory of my parents, Esther and Milton Edelman

Contents

Part One

Part Two

Part Three

Part Four

and over all the houses a melody will gather the scattered words
like a hand gathering crumbs upon a table

—Yehuda Amichai

Part One

Dream of the Gone-From City

The problem in the dream is to get home at night
without a car, a wallet or a cent in your pocket.

A route scrolls out like black and white film inside your head—
the boulevard you'll have to walk—a bulked up arm stretched

miles across the darkened sprawl: through canyon walls of offices
gone black behind their glass, tunnels under freeways, long blanks

of parks, projects abandoned to their boarded up stories, blocks
where roots erupt through sidewalk, where there are no roots,

no sidewalk; paint-stripped houses in raggy skirts of weeds, street
devoid of cars, stoplights gone meaningless as misplaced punctuation.

Now: the blurred fast cut, the double image. You're on the street,
walking with your loud heart. Like every other time, you watch yourself

turn into a dark shortcut. Skinny street, walled in, it's three a.m.,
and all that intersects is tunnel-like and winding. Shadows solidify

to figures crouched just around corners. How could you choose this again
and again? Why take the risk? To step into this vicious little detour—

no mace, no money, no image of the home you're walking toward.

Twins

Two blond boys walk
toward one another, unaware,
along the right-angled walls
of a block of building
at whose corner I wait
like a resolving chord.

Stop.
I speak it just before they collide.

They have become young men
on a white screen, blank
but for the wedge of building
and my obelisk shadow
pointing toward it.

Look at one another—
You're identical.

But they are not
anymore. The face of one
molds through variations
on the theme of the other
and settles finally on gentle parody
(conveyed through lips
and the slant of eyebrows).

The men smile shyly at each other, edging back—
the white air charged
with what has almost happened.

*

If I walk at right angle,
or obliquely, toward the person
I might have been,
will she acknowledge me?
Or pin her gaze on something
urgent, just beyond my head?

I have not lived
inside the dark house
between us, spying through curtains
on her lovers and her shoes,
bobbing in the wake
of her significant contralto.

If I approached that house
and peered into each window,
I might articulate a different
twin in every room.

Evening Song

My mother is short, my mother is bent,
my mother is sick of living.
My mother is alive, my mother is in pain,
my mother is quick, my mother is funny.
Mother of multiplied shrinkage—
less sight, less hearing, less husband, less husband,
my mother talks
when she feels like it, goes deaf
when she doesn't.
She didn't need to get old
to do exactly what she wants. She loves kids, loves babies, loves
other people's kids and babies. My mother's still
sharp, still hungry,
still awake when she's awake. Let's face it,
she's a marvel, a maze, I'm amazed
that she can still feel marvel: at the lilacs,
the ducks, at the purple-gray weight of the storm cloud
distending. She'd just rather be dead, that's all.
She still wants me to visit, to accept gifts, to quit
mumbling, to put the milk away, to scratch
her back, to go to hell, to come back soon. She's stubborn,
stubborn as a groundhog, as a brown spot,
stubborn as a sore that won't heal and now a second
on the left leg.
Stubborn as a deaf old woman in a white Chevy truck
who sees double and keeps on driving.

Vacant Rooms at Hotel Infinity

We gather in a lodge with room stacked on hidden room, like gaps among branches of spruce. The cat is small again and in my pocket. I'm small again and in parentheses.

A moonless field: my father names the constellations. The sky has more stories than the library! The swan that ate the scorpion that bit the hunter that shot the centaur. The dipper that led the slaves northward—it filled their drinking gourds with wine and drowned their enemies.

"How far up does the sky go?"
"Forever," he says, "That's called infinity."
"It has to stop somewhere."
"Where?"
"When it hits the ceiling."
"Then what's on the other side of that ceiling?" he says.

I crouch and grab tufts of wet grass. The earth is spinning in forever. I could be flung out like a spore.

Forever is time, not space. Does space only go on in time? Time can go on in a very small room with tall shadows and light seeping in through the door crack.

The sky today is like gray insulation. The cat is like gray insulation. She makes rooms beneath chairs and tables, in cupboards and boxes and bags.

I drew a ceiling on top of the sky and a room above and another
ceiling and another room and so on because I could not imagine
infinity without partitions I could not conceive of the sky not stopping
so I made it stop again and again and imagined instead an infinity of
stopping an infinity of ceilings and rooms and rockets tearing holes
in the ceilings and stars trapped and gathered along the edges like
iridescent moths.

For Patti

I don't know what killed you
so I say it was the old, wild life
come knocking.

I hadn't seen you since Catate, Petaluma,
Santa Rosa in skin white as hospital walls,
eyes dropped back deep and gone solid.
Patti, my absent, absent one.

Before that, we're thirteen
in the nowhere of our Bible
Belt town: black sky, black
highway, black lake.

Patti, my nineteen-sixties, my freight train
howl, my cow town shit hole, my one neon
Main Street, my girls' room Kools, my smuggled
fifths, my conned hooch, my under-the-bleachers
feels, my pay phone bomb scares, my swords
into plowshares, my tear gas parades, my cornfield
arrests, my fifteen, sixteen

my arm in arm partner
into dark water.

The River

Trucks on either side of us like fists, like cities.

Steep green against the highway. Cows
and caved-in, slat-gray shanties

Someone hung her voice up on a hook.

Willows dip their limbs in the shallows
Shall we gather, shall we gather, shall we

Blue cracks in the plaster sky and
everything opening along the road:
violets, trillium, azalea, the guts of deer

have become one.

I'm not in my body yet, she said. *As if without skin*, she said. *Not solid.*
Like this, and she opened a book by a painter
who renders herself as skinless.

"How do I know I'm not a brain in a vat?" says the skeptic.

"Because I have two hands," says the empiricist.

At the rest stop men are like trucks, their bulk set
smack   in the center of the walk, enormous boots.

We have to cut among them   their talk
washes us like exhaust fumes.

Transparent. Fizzing into halves. Made of thin stuff that
splits and unravels.   Flaps.

So much darkness around it, so much mist.   Night woods
thick with the wing song of insects.   Wide bend
       on a night with no moon, no wind. Surface disturbed,
                                   the water
    rolled out the notes of its logic.

Red and the memory of red.   *Trans-parented.*

"Because people stare at my breasts," says the empiricist.

Some a' that, piece a' that, check that, hit that.

That skank. She could have refused those photos. Those poses.
    She was *smiling.*

*Why fight   when you could leave your skin and watch
    from a distance—the pressure-cooked face, the antics
of the amped-up body—too ridiculous to fight.*

    The altered syntax of her limbs.

The fast water giveth and the fast water

                              Red-winged blackbirds
                                    spiral above the river

       Rocks smooth as skin beneath the rapids
Amen.

The highway climbs
          between the old-god faces of blasted out rock

Trucks have a long blind spot   Pass them fast.

Look downward, the valley breathes, languorous
                                        and deep.

The river's a knife in its green sheath.

The Lost Poem

Why does this written doe bound through these written woods?
—Wislawa Szymborska

I'd stuck it in a mental cubbyhole, then all the cubbyholes
filled up with rice and shoes. Maybe this is how it went:

I found a pencil with an actual point and looked for paper.
The dryer buzzed. I took the clothes out. As I was folding them

the phone rang. I said hello, hello? The silence opened
like a sheet of paper. Was it a robot or a murderer?

*

There once lived a girl in a Soho loft
with hair like a two-story warehouse.

By her phone, she hung a chrome
whistle. Who was it that rang and rang

and would not speak? Did the numbers
he touched become points on her body?

The rings and the pauses between them her
breathing? And what of the shriek of whistle?

*

I woke to say, of course. No need to write it down,
it's obvious. The poem had a dampness
and a list. Or was I sweating in the dream?

A movie clings to me for days now. Men with rifles
and no masks. The poem did not have all that
moonlight and blood. The poem had no horses.

*

The woods below my home are white, their fragile branches
lined in ice. The road is neither field nor road. Deer tracks

pock the snow as far as I can see. Gunshots from the lower slope. I put
the whistle to my lips. The poem lurches through the iced branches.

Maple Grove

They put him in the left wing but by then he lacked a sense of
serendipity, or irony. He enjoyed the words, though. Sinister nurses.
Window on the parking lot. He no longer drove. He'd lost his mind

sometimes. It came back for visits and left like the rest of us.
Then he lost his last name. The first shall be the last
also. Did they think he wouldn't know himself as Edelman?

Professor? Mister? They had time for one syllable: Milt.
They were underpaid. So there went his parents, brothers,
kids, adulthood. What's in a family name? Everything

stank. Real flowers smelled like plastic. He no longer walked. He
was not often pleasant. He'd lost his heart's sweetness, sometimes.
Of course he preferred the past. He could get there on his own

for one thing: the icehouse at Lily Lake, where he hid with his
twin on hot afternoons. Like this one, the one in which he
tells me that story, coaxed out for minutes into blessed shade.

Then he explains hydraulic brakes. I think the growling was
involuntary. After a long snarl, he'd sigh, "OK." Getting it
all out, I guess. Like when he said, "Piss, Shit." A man who

never swore, who never liked my mother's cussing in her two
mother tongues (though he admired her flair for juxtaposition).
He was passing through stages like a toddler, learning language

as he lost it. I buzzed the nurse: "My father's gurgling." "Gurgle,"
said my father, traveling backward toward the first spring of sound.
Jerry O'Malley visited daily. "Milton Edelman!" He said it on arrival

and departure. "Jerry O'Malley!" said my father to his friend, learning
that to name the whole person is to hold him, fast, throughout
the arc of his translation; to reconstitute him daily at the heart's table.

Tunnel Road

Obsession is the opposite of creativity
                —LJ

If I look all day into a face
that may be there
or not there,

I enter a tunnel.

If I look all day into a face that is itself a tunnel,
I enter
        A)   a windowless room
        B)   a windowless room

There was so much snow that there was only snow,
and spruce trunks black in snow,
and glide of Nordic skis on snow,
and silence
like a bridge of ice between two continents.

There was a road called Tunnel Road
we never found,
a mated set of tracks we never saw,
a warming hut we never reached,
a fire inside the hut.

At the hut we never reached, a man
and woman park their skis and enter

to a wood stove, table, iron poker, axe,
light through two small windows.

She stokes the fire. He throws on logs.
She takes off gloves, then boots.

He watches her undress. He thinks
each layer must be the last,
but there's another, and another.

We drew two stories through the hush of woods,
amid the faintest bird tracks, the iced rivulets,
the Hemlocks dressed as polar bears.

We took turns burrowing through powder,
or gliding in the other's tracks. The snow
was falling now, or circling, climbing.

Our hair was filled with jewels,
our tracks erasing.

Part Two

Adirondacks, May

Let it be night when you plunge
on wheels through the ravenous
forest. Bats, ecstatic, twist
into illumined view and shoot upward;
the lewd-faced possum trails
his nude tail into the spotlight
of your high beams.
At the bend, there, nibbling, the doe
bares her throat to your oncoming glare,
tracks you sideways in the gaze of her one eye
in light. And you see that it's your own
slow longing she's captured—in the neck,
the tongue, in the lithe, submissive body.
Let the trees claw at wind. The moon,
half occluded, is your lost eye
opening; the road is a nerve stem
through hemispheres of trees
and your taut rabbit heart
is the double blade of light
calling out to the dark.

What She Taught Me

My mother taught me to take back what was rotten, stale, or tasteless and to expect an apology along with a refund. She taught me to walk in boy's shoes, to ride a bike with a bar, to smirk back at smirkers, to kick anyone who snickered. She hit me with a yardstick. She taught me to play ball, taught me to hit, to drive from the hips and swing, then lay down the bat like a daffodil. She taught me to run, to throw like a boy. She taught me to tell everyone to go to hell. She told me to go to hell. She taught me to drive when I was nine. She taught me to serve the men first. With her back to me, she taught me to adore my brothers, to mirror my sister, to pity the girl who stalked my sister in hallways to call her *Jew*. She taught the whole town to compost, how to vote, to abort their unwanted young. She taught me to pull weeds at the root. She taught me not to say shit at the table. She taught me to say shit. She taught me songs. She taught me I couldn't sing. She taught me to love my body. She taught me I was loved for my body. She taught me to fold the napkin once and place the fork on it, to dampen the dust mop, to let the pan sit in cold water, to pull the skin off a chicken, to carry spiders outside alive, to hang suet, scatter corn on the stoop for titmice, wrens, chickadees; to laugh at the gathering of crashers—fat squirrels, chipmunks, rabbits; to love the muted beauty of the female cardinal in bright sunlight.

Geometry Problem

I pass the sunset, squared
inside the gleaming steel side
of a southbound truck. Encapsulated,
I have passed to the other side—heaven
is motion, what babies know,
drooling through whole states.

Blessed am I, when neither
here nor there. What I can't
touch won't hurt me.

And what do these buzzards
in their slow circles know,
these topless isosceles
triangles? I have forgotten
the Pythagorean theorem.
Their slight V's
are the devil's eyebrows.

Pea brains! Who are you
to know something I don't,
aloft beneath a lost
hypotenuse?

Ohio slides by me and the land
flattens into Indiana where gas
is cheap and you pump first.

At each stop, truckers munching
Snickers get bigger. Six and a half
feet from felt hats to snakeskin toes;
giant buckles prop up their plaid

stomachs. I want to ride
with them forever.

The low sun thins into winter. I have a mother
at the end of this road, she's stirring pea soup
as dusk thickens around her house.

And my father draws each blind, crooks
a finger through the wooden
ring at the tip of each string, pulls
a blank on his own reflection.

Cardinal Flight

The male cardinal bashes his brains against his own
territoriality. Modest wife with an orange mouth.

They've nested in the pin oak. He cracks sunflower
seeds and slides them into her throat. In the alternate

oak of my guest room window, a second male alights,
defiant in sunlight, and so the first makes a missile

of his crimson self, zooms at the intruder, falls
stunned by his own driven image. The man who

explicates this drama, via phone from his remote
domain, goes back to his canvas: to self-portraits

he builds like beautiful tombstones, layer on razored
layer of paint; to immense female figures that are also

self-portraits, whose eyes bite back, whose nipples
point back at the hand that carves them. He won't

intervene with the cardinal drama by lowering
a blind, as I do now, but lets birds suicide dive

against the excellent windows he's designed around
himself. *The smartest will survive and breed.*

The rest keep flying at him, lured by a misread
reflection—the glare of their own hunger.

Waiting Room/Christmas Eve

There's seasonal art on the orthopedist's walls—
faux wrapped gifts the size of flattened bathtubs,

pattern of gilded starfish sparkling in sand.
Image of the image   of the star   of the fish.

A gold bow explodes dead center: birth of a sun
into 3D. Oprah's on the cover of *Oprah*. A woman

in a reindeer sweater says Oprah will take over
social security and give us each nine thousand dollars.

The newspaper says soldiers in Afghanistan who exhibit
symptoms such as *I don't think I can do it again*   *I don't*

think I can do it again   are required to seek counseling.
A big man in work boots and paint splattered jeans

signs in with a bandaged hand. "Employer information?"
The receptionist smiles like a gift you can't unwrap.

He lists for her   employer's name, phone, address, zip
by heart like a prayer. The faith in his recitation breaks

inside my throat, edge of an ocean. O star spangled
sand. O room where we sit with skin on our bones,

with smiles and photos of smiles.

The Carriage House

For years I've returned in sleep to a guesthouse on an alley that smelled of eucalyptus where a blond girl walked her little son to school and home each day. I moved across the country but can't seem to exit that home—elflike and low in a culture of sun—where inside and outside were hard to divide, where ivy tightened around the stucco frame, oak door, casement windows, walled-in yard, the ancient swing.

I think that I live in two places at once, a spacious one by day and the dollhouse I return to like a ghost at night, that I enter without key, without cost; that someone else inhabits now though as a dreamer I can't see her. Some nights I move the guesthouse to the middle of a wood, and some nights thieves stand in shadows at the broken back door.

What is it I can't let go of? The person I think I was when I lived there? I gave the little boy my stuffed bear and left, wishing I had something for the other child, his mother.

I wake and carry my divided self through day. Relief of green slope: of locusts, hemlocks, oaks; my porch, my cat, my several rooms; the cry of a young hawk repeated.

Algebra Problem

The branches of bare sumac draw X's and Y's
across a white sky and I think of Algebra II,
the stroke upon stroke of wrong turns that multiplied
how lost I got. My father sat down and worked with me.
At fifteen I started learning for the first time how to fail
at learning and garner his rare attention. By year's
end I could barely add without a tutoring session.

His desk was an oak door laid across file cabinets,
and his patience like a second door that swung into
an unfamiliar room. He gripped a yellow pencil and, one
scrap of paper at a time, unveiled to me equations inside
the equations, until I felt I could rebuild our house
from its foundation up with those fleshless X's and Y's—
my brief grasp of a universe that fit perfectly together—
my father almost reachable across his fence of numbers.

Bordeaux

The house fills up with the young and expat hip. They buy their clothes at thrift stores. They can sleep anywhere. You haven't had a shower. Your stuff is scattered all over. They sometimes break down into individuals but then the individuals are interchangeable. For example, there's Emma. There were two of her but when you look very closely, you think, yes, that's Emma, and the other who looked like her becomes someone else, but still a little bit Emma. And Emma says only things that are big, about China and Time. And because you want something from her, you nod and say, *yes, yes, China, Time*—so you can then go on to ask the thing you want from her, something like, *Where's the bathroom?* Or, *which bus will get me to the Gare de Bordeaux Saint-Jean?* Or, *what's happened to all my stuff?* Because as usual, your fragments are strewn about the house—your T-shirts, jeans, sandals—the paraphernalia of your face—your sticks and tubes and brushes and pouches and creams. But when she finally stops for breath and you get to ask your question, the thing you want from her, the reason you've listened to China and Time, Emma says, *No, let's sit with this first.* And you must. Because her skin is flawless and she wears her scarf a certain way. And because she's talking about big things and you're talking about lipstick, or the loo, or the train you have to catch to get where you're going next.

Assisted Living

Her phone is like a cordless baby. Her children
are a blur of programmed digits. Each week she
writes new algorithms to survive, from toothbrush

to spoon. Her softball glove, her Raleigh 3 speed
are not even memory. Her new sports are dress,
food, hygiene. A slalom course to every doorknob.

A daughter's like a banister or vice versa. She's lost
her League of Women Voters' calendar. There may be
scribbled meetings, names sweet as cherries left to rot

in a place where she can't smell them. Somewhere
in the ivy there's a dead animal, alive with a scent
she's starting to enjoy, almost enough to roll in

and howl. Every cell an insurrection. Every misheard
word a revolution. The house isn't gone yet. It isn't there
either if she can't get inside. All the hard-won scabs

and treasures, the family of objects, are stacking up in churches
and thrift stores, in neighbors' garages, in lists her children carry.
Every daughter is an insurrection. She gets around as a resourceful

prisoner in the new place, sniffing out the secret exits, free diapers,
abandoned *New York Times* with puzzles she can half finish,
the paperback she can't see to read for more than seven minutes.

Cat Act

The cat thinks she's a child again. Christ.
Aren't I finally too old for this? She's
wearing sneakers, up on her hind legs,

banging on the windows with a stick.
She's dying to get out of my house,
out from under my opposable thumb.

What a stupid cartoon I've created. What
a child with no interior. But strong—
she could whack me with that stick or bite me.

She's gotten *really* tall. Now she's in my arms,
an infant/cat with an eight-year-old's voice.
"You shouldn't be wearing those shoes," I say.

"Why not?" she says, all plaintive. "Because—
you're a cat." (I hate telling her that).
"Well, I like wearing them. They're Pumas."

I guess I have to let her. Let her be who she is
and all that crap. Anyway, how could I stop her?
She'll just grow tall again and find another stick.

I notice now she's taking on a very tawny hue.
A guy shows up. He has a careful handsomeness
that I find ugly. But he becomes another child—

a grown-up child with a big, doughy face.
Insists he'll be responsible for the cat.
Wants to schlep her in her baby pack

to some sticky theater where he regains his
face and argues shit with other men. Of course
he loses her. Doesn't even know what building

he was in. (Had to be a building, she's an indoor
cat.) I yell into his thick face but he's impermeable.
I scream out weeks and months of grief; the dough

just thickens. He won't tell me even if he knows.
Meanwhile, the cat could be dead by now.

North of Sunset

in memory of Joel

The night is at the point of running over
　　—Octavio Paz

We took disco lessons in a Malibu living room
　　open deck on the Pacific　　　　　　　counter boom of surf on cliffs.

I learned to lead　　　from a follow position.
Joel's lead　　　was a ghost touch　　　his sense of rhythm
　　hypothetical.

I was the skirt　　　but he the ingénue
　　black lashes over violet eyes

closing　　　on yet another sunset where
　　everyone is warm　　　where even the toes of the homeless
　　　　troll forgiving sand.

He never went homeless　　　in the end　　　friends took him in　　　his skin
　　a bloom of violets.

Sittin' here eatin' my heart out, waitin',
Waitin' for some lover to call,
Dialed about a thousand numbers, lately,
Nearly yanked the phone off the wall

I held his fingers and twirled he might have been a silk scarf
　　　　might have been a wife, a father　　　a mogul in a Rolls.

He disappeared
      whole birthday parties followed
            Sometimes they fill my living
                  room, their cadences and faces.

Sun enough for everyone   though in Malibu it might be
     afternoon
        before the world assumes a shape
          the fog hangs thick with tricks.

    Walk out into the dropped cloud of morning   the sea is thundering
      as if above you   under you
         and you have no idea where the shore drops off.

The Writing of Desire

I had to go because I wrote my middle name.
I wrote it in the sand with a stick and then I
screamed in circles like a gull.
You stared down and stared
and then you knelt
and traced it in the sand with your finger—
        deep, past the second knuckle.
I had to go.
The red sun slipped
toward the ocean
        like a kiss.

The tide would take the cove.
We named the waves, they came to us
in families of seven.
I wanted to stay with you until I grew
gills. I wanted to stay
until the fish walked out and shook our hands.
I had to go because I wrote my middle name,
and the red sun hung
above the ocean
        like a bullet wound.

I wrote it in the sand with a stick.
You saw it
and the sea would take it
and you'd watch.

I had to climb the rocks that hid us,
        the red sun hung.
I had to burn along the sand that ate my footprints,
        I wrote my middle name.

I had to tear across the salty tongues of foam,
I had to leave you
kneeling in the cove
gold and shining. And the sun hissed
red into the ocean.

Part Three

The monster might be your own memory, wild horses, your mother who can breathe air but who doesn't want to, who goes down instead, who seeks the deepest trench, the one unmeasured, carved by the glacier that dug this lake, then melted to fill it.

—Melanie Rae Thon

Dead Languages

I have memories, you know.
I'm not a person with a helium
balloon for a head.

I rode my bike home
from swimming practice
and ate watermelon.

I ate the melon on the stoop,
sliced it into smiles and spit
the seeds into the grass.

At practice I traveled
between atmospheres
with the rotation of my head.

Fast crawl. My face and lips
loving the supple border
of air and water,

my left ear turning
in and out of the loud
silence of submersion.

I can't remember anything else.
I've always pictured the week
as a warped circle of linked

asymmetrical spaces, the name
for each day printed in a space
like a state on a map.

Each day is a slightly different
color but all of the colors drab.

Exposure I

I was talking to a shrink about lack of focus she said here's an extreme example a woman cleaning her house who stops scrubbing the sink to get a rag from the closet and from there sees she'd started dusting the bedroom and stopped to get cleanser from the kitchen so she resumes dusting the bedroom forgetting the kitchen until she walks to the bathroom to dampen the dustcloth and sees the cabinet open and empty and remembers she'd been cleaning the cabinet when she went to the kitchen to get cleanser and noticed she'd been scouring the sink when

In fact the therapist said only a few of these words and I plugged myself right in I am that extreme example I said but are you sure it slows my cleaning and she said Ah but the woman cleaning is a metaphor a capsule of actual behavior thus literal speed of metaphorical cleaning is irrelevant and I thought then of cleaning as metaphor for therapy a monolog confined to one room within a circumscribed time and would a portion of my brain be cleaner when I emerged

I thought of monolog as metaphor for type A cleaning and of my more expansive style as dialog among all rooms which are rooms of the self another shrink told me when I dreamed the delicious dream of more and more rooms opening up off my one room apartment—more space! I rejoiced but he said No more parts of the self and I loved that too my very selves as multiplying square footage and then he said More parts of Barbara! and when he did that third person thing I thought several things all at once

> Oh God, he's one of those

> If his face were gigantic it would make an excellent climbing wall

> Is he talking about some other Barbara and if so what's the point of extra rooms if I have to share?

Girl in a Coonskin Cap, Circa 1953

for Kerry

Only her sneakers face the camera. She's three,
poised for a stump speech on a flipped bucket,
a heart sewn into the bib of her overalls. The plump

cheeks beam. Fantastic animal hairdo! It lifts her
three inches. The striped tail adorns her shoulder
like she grew it herself. All around, the outskirts

of a Michigan town she'll later dub *Bland Vapids*.
The flatlands. Her body swivels west, toward
the Rockies she's just invented in all their strata,

down to the three billion-year-old core. Then east,
toward the Appalachians, whose white mists rise
out of gorges like sketches of lives she might one day

muscle into color. So much to investigate and dissect.
Before the classroom's sealed windows and its infant crawl
toward afternoon, toward the far edge of the Fifties.

The frontiers are out there, in the narratives of arrowheads
and bones, the alternating currents of the brain, the body's
sweet topography. Mick Jagger, thank God, is not far

around the corner. And Grace Slick will arrive at the
White House for Tricia Nixon's Fiske women's tea, hiding six
hundred micrograms of acid to spike the president's drink.

*

Meanwhile the sky is a milk-based soup. Behind the baby face
so full of appetite and savvy, chicken wire rises to the height
of her cap, then a long block of barracks like a stuck train,

then phone poles—a line of double crosses.

Bee Movies

Monoculture. n. 1. cultivation of a single crop within a farm, region, country;
2. a single, homogeneous culture

Key words: Pistil, Wistful, You're gonna miss me, honey

I
A woman dances in a shirt of live bees,
arms upraised in their pulsing sleeves,
the sky behind her a cerulean whole note.

II
O disappearing bees
Why are your bodies never found?
You abandon your eggs, your queen,
you leave the flower to its torched outpost.

> "And I, of ladies most deject and wretched,
> That sucked the honey of his music vows."

III
A scientist keeps me on his B list for Bee movies.
His colleagues talk through me, embarrassed
by my floral print. I stand critiqued by their
T shirts from commendable events.

> "Like sweet bells jangled, out of tune . . ."

IV
Drones and workers, we've deposed your queen
and propped up a younger one. No more pumpkin,
no more buckwheat. Everywhere you fly now,
cherries—days and nights of cherries. And for the year's
remainder, we'll shoot you full of high fructose corn syrup.

V

The notion of meadow is a searing nostalgia.

VI

Here's the empirical evidence:

> a) The king is in the countinghouse, counting out his money
> b) The queen is in the parlor, eating bread and honey

The keeper keeps a mobile hive, a box of sticky
shelves in which the colony is trucked across
the continent, to pollinate each crop in its brief season

Each stratum to its region
> hard science in the front row
> drones and workers in the middle, too numerous to count
> poets in the bowls of their hunger

VII

Conclusions

> ". . . for so work the honeybees,
> Creatures that by a rule in nature teach
> The act of order to a peopled kingdom."

Meadows of clover, vetch, daisies—
each petal holds the memory
of contact.

I lack the courage of the bee shirt.
I lack appropriate solemnity, acuity.

He will appropriate my tune, my sentences
that break the skin; he'll vanish
with his head full of maps, his iris magnified
like sky
on muscular legs, with precision
fingers, his calm like gold
in the face of crisis, his mind
in clean, hexagonal cells.

Intersection

Driving toward a school north of Pittsburgh, above me
stoplights swing in wind, strung across a highway
that strings together three dead mill towns.

Years ago, a passenger, I watched stoplights
bounce from their black cords as wind reached in to us
through open windows. "That's always an oddly lonely sight," I said.

"Peculiar to America," said my friend. "They don't hang lights
like that elsewhere." I felt us both suspended then. He was peculiar

to America. I thought that he was lonely no matter
where he went and so was I. That each of us moved
and stopped in the places we stopped and
moved inside some precarious belief in how we were

supposed to live. And then the light changed. And then
he went back to Tel Aviv, in a year when the movement toward
peace in his region felt possible and huge.

The light tips bottom-up inside its yellow
casement, the red lit shiny as a city I can't
reach and I forget where I'm going or what it is

I'm meant to do there while
above me the rules destabilize.

Exposure II

The hematologist wants to freeze us.
Sixty minutes in this public refrigerator,
the blood stops moving. For the first time,
I connect two meanings of the word *patient*.

My mother's shirt's inside out. "Your teeth
are so white," she says loudly. Now the other
hypothermic patients have something to do—
pretend they're not listening. She's lost

her artificial tears. I hand her mine
and she knocks back a shot
in each eye. "What did you pay for these?
I get mine for 89 cents at Walmart."

No one else is talking now. We look out
through glass walls at baked asphalt.
Enter a woman with a stroller. "A boy?
How wonderful!" says my mother. "How much

does he weigh? What did he weigh at birth?"
I could be twelve again, six, nineteen:
a girl smashing glass inside a statue
of a girl sitting perfectly still. "Let's wait

outside," she says. I give her my arm.
The sun hits us like a shovel. Ducks
waddle at the edge of the asphalt.
Then a square, carved pond like a

dead TV screen. A forest of poplars
once grew here. I conjure them—numerous,
immense, casting layers of undulating
shade. My mother sighs. She feels them too.

Shopping at Ross Dress for Less

In for the quick kill.
I'll get this over with and be clothed
and fool people.
A sound cuts into my purpose, a diphthong
twists and rises from a child.

Or it's a Siamese cat
in the body of a child
leaning from a shopping cart.
¿Hiiieee? ¿Hiiieee?

She unfolds the rolls of her arm
toward the troops of ruffled dresses, clasps
and unclasps her slow fingers
¿Hiiieee?

The headless dresses do not answer.
The limp sleeves do not wave back.
Close, I hear the mother speaking,
¡Cállate! ¡Siéntate!

So it's a Spanish word, *hay*—
but it's a question, *Is there? Is there?*
¿hay? ¿hay? ¿hay?
Is there what?

Is there a Santa Claus?
Is there a God?
Is there a difference between people and clothes?
Is there anything left to say?
Is there? Is there?
¿Aaiiee? ¿Aaiiee?

The syllable lifts and hangs
among the empty dresses
suspended from their metal question marks.

Cloud Father

"What's down the toilet?" I asked,
flushing five times, transfixed
by the magical swirl.

"Never Never Land,"
he answered. "Stop
wasting water."

We flew to Urbana
on a DC-3—
a winged hippopotamus
bumping toward extinction—
through the light and dark cauliflower
thunder clouds.

"Is that a dirty book?"
I said at the airport.

"No. They put this picture on it
so that people will buy it."

"Well, what's the book about?"

"I don't know.
I bought it for the picture."

I may have made that story up
the way I make him up now,
the way I dream him
into foolishness—
the father who finally wants me—
he doesn't know better,

so I must
kiss his forehead,
as he did mine when
I was a child. His dream skin
is like old cheese.

And when he speaks
his blither of syllables
I put my arms around him
and he starts to form words,
to tell me
what he wants from me.

Then I remember
I am dreaming him,

that when we speak on the phone—
his voice rumbling, fixed
inside the storm's eye of logic—

he will forget
the names of my friends,
what I've written, the little
tucked tail of my accomplishments,

but he'll remember
the delicate topography of clouds
the storms they gave birth to

altostratus
cumulonimbus
cirrus nothus
cirrostratus nebulosus

All the Doomed Swimmers

The weekend he arrived, hornets
swarmed at my window, flattened
their wings like a glistening
skin and slid through a gap
in the screen to get at us.

When ten of them circled the kitchen
we started swinging. The fastest
headed for the track lights and fried.
I still find their scorched carcasses.

All the clocks in my house are wrong—
flat hands, flat faces,
the little bastards tick like accidents.

Outside now, kamikaze snowflakes dive
and melt on wet ground, cloud my vision.
Icicles drip and glisten. Another sigh.
Another towel stiffens in the hamper.

It was hot when we would not touch.
We danced in dark crowds, bumped up
against strangers. Oblong sweat drops
sledded down my body.

Somewhere along the sizzling river
we kissed, then our tongues became
fish, each of us will-less, unraveling
into one cluttered river—with its
paddle wheels and clowns and downed
stars, its Styrofoam and carp, its
barges and rust and wet blues.

Everything swims, like the protein
clouds that float through my lover's
iris, the stars in his paintings with
blurred tails; they blink, swim
out of frame, and I
ache like the empty spaces
of their constellations.

One Story

for my mother

That's not my stomach rumbling,
it's yours.

I didn't say that song
reminds me of a truck backing up—
that's a thought
you created in my voice. I didn't say

your shoulders remind me of the Washington Arch
but they do
and the arc inside the square is one story
of your body

and your gait reminds me of a truck
backing up, and the red spot on your leg
reminds me of a helium balloon I let go of in the St. Louis railroad
station, I was four, it rose to the top of the dome
and stuck there like a ladybug.

I read on the wall of an underpass,
"Memory is a divided tree."

I remember words that floated
through the dome of the station. I remember
walking out without my red balloon
into the slurry and the slush, and seeing
that a city is a field of moving legs

where cars and buses rumble
as my stomach has been rumbling,

as your thoughts have rumbled quietly
in others' voices

Your thoughts are wonderful
and many-colored. They've traveled like hot air
balloons through all the years you've lived.

Your voice
is a divided tree. I've stood
between its whole trunks
listening,
roots to darkened sky.

Part Four

It is nor hand nor foot in mouth

Forgot to type your name, forgot how to say it, forgot the sound of it, I mean the spell of it, forgot how to spell it, forgot you had a name, forgot you had a face below your hair above your earrings, forgot the meaning of your name, forgot how to mean it, forgot your name means stranger, *Barbara*, which is strange because you're so familiar, you're like family, I call you by my daughter's name, her name is Rosemary, you're like a spice to me, a bloom, you're like a virgin, I call my daughter by her mother's name, that fiend, you're like a mother to me, you're like Helen Mirren in *The Queen,* no, scratch that, Helen Mirren's like *my* mother in *The Queen,* we saw it in an empty theater, you walked along the bannister, you're like a cat to me, an acrobat, you're like *Prime Suspect* Helen Mirren. Forgot the root of your name, forgot its trunk, its limbs, its tender intersections.

Two Weeks

White hydrangea   real ones my mother grew   Plastic vase
    plastic diapers on the shelf   His face grows skeletal
arms still muscular

    If they move even his arm   he yells that he'll fall out of bed
      A machine and two aids haul him bellowing into his wheelchair

    I read him Saul Bellow   Faulkner   *Get your car let's go home*   He's
    forgotten that he stopped walking   stopped standing

He's walking the edge of something   in his barred bed   he's falling
    right hand an enormous blossom   a blown-up float
           sacred river

Say the first lines of "Kubla Khan," Dad   his spine a drooping stem
He sees it's a test   rallies   to the full punch
           my father the cooperative child

Down   *to a sunless sea*   *Cover me I'm cold*

    The Owl and the Pussy-cat went to sea
     In a beautiful pea-green boat
   They took some honey, and plenty of money
     Wrapped up in a five-pound note

    I got him to recite it long after I'd learned it myself

He loved the sounds of nonsense verse   rhymes that are layered like
birthday cakes   memory mammary mummery   caverns
measureless to man

I read him "Gimpel the Fool"   the room a cavern of demons

He fell asleep and I stopped and I watched
and he woke and I read and he slept
and I stopped and he dreamed he was dead
and he woke and said *I'm dead*
and then *Keep reading*

Something Is Digging

Everything was fine until one stray hour
cracked the afternoon open and the day

began to eat its own tail. I met the one-suit
duo with a river view. They'd worked up a skit

for me: good cop, bad apple; i.e., find another
tree. I had no stone, no flame, no black magic

marker to stake my inviolate claim. What seeped
through the fissure was a plague of lists to be addressed:

weed, shine, lie, propagate. Lists bubble up in
dreams and cluster around my head in waking:

stick, graft, pluck, mother. Catch up. Pollen dusts
the dark water. Leaves rust like abandoned shovels.

Something is digging in perpetuity: for grubs, nuts,
blood, shelter. The lilies have been strangled,

the geraniums beheaded; the synchronous
bugs are munching everything I've worked for.

Go West

At ninety-two she'll move to Hollywood,
shrugging off the ground
        of seven decades—the dirt she worked—
Midwestern fertile crescent of mispronounced Egyptian names:

its cliffs and wooded hills, its lakes
        with their attendant herons, ducks,
bald eagles that return to winter nests,
the cardinals and finches at her feeder,
        the rows of corn and soy
and headstones.

        How much of this landscape is still active in her system?

Her life in Southern Illinois has shrunk
        to a few faces, fewer rooms, a pool, a list of numbers,
humidity that holds her like a pair of arms,
a chair looking out on a mown field,
        the visitations of the ruby-throated hummingbird.

No one visits. Those who do talk too much. Laugh at things
        that aren't funny. They don't enunciate.
They inflect each statement as if it were a question.

        Go West, old woman.

It's not her first migration. She typed her way through war
in mukluks on a Kodiak Island naval base—
        her flight from all that was familiar.

The promise now is sunshine and blood.
She'd looked toward death as her next big
        adventure. Or her escape from joint pain.

Her sons kick in like firemen:
          one to nudge her out, the other waiting
with a net. Aloft, she circles ocean, freeways,
mountains with their dirty skirts, the city's fabric
          stitching into the brown hem of sky in three directions.

She wakes to a birdless world, to the strange drone of traffic.

And to red clay roofs, to balconies of bougainvillea spilling
over wrought iron. What do you remember, *vecchia,* of the *Mediterraneo?*
          i balconi, i tetti rossi come questi?

There's music that isn't Christian, food that isn't fried,
tai chi in wheelchairs, smatterings of Yiddish, performers
          just a step-ball-change from Broadway,
orange trees in planters, their bright fruit ripe for the plucking
          by anybody who can reach.

The pool is not a euphemism. It's a bathtub.

Visitors surge in and recede like the ocean she never sees.
          For eighty minutes daily, the sun lights up the concrete courtyard.

Visit with Aunt Eve

She used a cane but moved very fast
like water that circumvents all obstacles—
curb, stairs, people,

threshold. We sat on the white sofa.
"I feel as though I have nothing to tell you,"
she said, and laughed.
I listened for a cadence of fear
in the tail of her laugh.

"Will you come back?" she asked.
"Yes."
"How do you like work?" she asked.
"Have you made a retirement plan?"
"Will you come back?"
"How's work?"

She embarked on each question
with the old, bright inflection;
she cracked the window
to her intelligent self but could not
enter the building;

or entered to find it had always
been bare—by which I mean,

has the sense of what she's lost
been also lost

and the term she's serving now
become a merciful one?—

a house in a meadow, without clutter;
and each time a bird
returns to the feeder,
it's the first time.

This cold night will turn us

My brother is suddenly jobless, impossible, he's the family genius, the physicist, two kids bound for college, big house on a lake, he says days are OK but nights he wakes sweating, it's twenty-five below in Minnesota, even the Malamute won't go out, he skis across a lake by day, the week before him shoreless.

In his LinkedIn photo he looks faded, I can't bear to connect him to the verb *network*, it has nothing to do with performance, they said, it's salary and age, you cost us too much, you and everyone like you, with your bald heads and metal hips, your long memories, your quaint loyalties.

Blizzard

January stamps its wet boot.
I miss the Pacific—furious,
submissive, the way it broods

or mutinies beneath an even sky;
the sun, exquisite and deadly on
my skin; the blue stupor of pools.

For ninety-six hours, snow has fallen
on the swollen rivers, the imprisoning
hills. My car's stuck in the Goodwill lot.

I give. I will them not to tow it. Then stumble
home along the white slot canyon of a
pounded path. I'll call it ice that keeps you

away tonight, but it's elements harder to
trace. When you were here I cooked, my
hands no longer my own, ownership revoked,

they tossed sauce red sauce on my pants,
shattered glass. I don't know whom they were
feeding. My index finger grins where I sliced

the top knuckle A blue bruise shaped like a
killer whale swims along the top of my
thumbnail. I breathed a wish, now see

how it descends: a calm night's sleep—
pristinely alone under a down quilt, snow
falling on the roof and ground and fire

escape; the space to move—in silence
from room to room, the long hours
opening around me like vowels.

Automatic Email Reply: Out of Office/Hospice

in memory of Carol Hamilton

How did the air change just then, she thought, and then lost the thought. The curdling light, the nervous screen, the ringing in her ears. Hard surfaces of tables spiked with metallic flecks.

A public buzz from inside the light or inside the screen, or maybe not a buzz at all, not a sound, but a flicker that feels like a buzz.

He had a buzz cut, said Aaron yesterday, looming over her after class, so you'd think he'd be like, some military guy, but he was like, *seedy*, I mean

What *do* you mean? She said.

I mean, like, seedy.

Well, how did you know? She said.

Know?

What about him was *seedy*? She said.

Well, he was like, you know, his clothes were two sizes too big and he pulled up his hood so you could barely see his face, and every crappy thing he had on was like, black or some other non-color.

What else? She said.

He was walking around with a WeedWacker, said Aaron.

But that was yesterday, she's sliding away from today, detouring into buzz cuts and WeedWackers, into anything but the actual *thing*.

Today is wet. This morning in Shakespeare the students wanted badly to be sleeping. Until she asked if they thought Bottom with his donkey head really wanted to *eat* those fairies Mustardseed and Peaseblossom rather than befriend them, and then all of their faces lifted, the private sleepiness of each like a screen door sliding open, and they stared as if *this*, as if *she* were the dream, and what they wanted badly now was to waken away from her.

In grad school the seminar table always made her hungry. In Celia's story, she'd said, the Thanksgiving turkey *is* the dead father. And her classmates stared the way the students this morning stared, but the prof, a man older than God, said, of course, they're carving the dead father and eating him with cranberry sauce.

But that's much further back than her earlier tangent, much further from the now of an hour ago that she's been sitting on like a bruise.

This afternoon in the wobbly light, in the inner ear ringing of a phone or doorbell that will not stop ringing, at the hesitant screen, in the grayish air, the sidewalks wet through arched windows, she scrolled by a subject line like a light blinking red through fog on a mountain road, and kept scrolling, didn't stop to open, thinking, maybe that's the name of an article C. is sending, or maybe it's one of her grim jokes, and then thinking, no, she doesn't do that anymore.

The Pedal-Duck Toy

In sleep I walk
along a big street in a small town
where I walked one night with my mother.
A starving wind inhabits the darkness.
It rips limbs from trees
to knock at every door
in search of the rest of itself.

I may have been eleven
but to the passing cars
I was another woman like her.
"What are they honking at?"
Her answer was a soft laugh
and I thought,
"She is no longer my mother."

Something's following me.
The first time I turn
there are three metal rings like giant
washers skidding in the wind. A gust
rights one of them and rolls it, a silver
sliver, into the maw
of darkened street.

The second time I turn for a person
but see a three-wheeled
plastic pedal-toy
shaped like a duck.
The child who was riding in it
blew into the sky, or there was
never a child inside

and the pedal-duck rolls empty behind me,
duck-face stuck in a soundless laugh
as the gaunt wind scavenges the pavement.

Mother of Bone

I don't have a system to measure
how dead you are now. You were
less dead at first, closer to surfaces.

At the malleable border of sleep
I heard your quilted voice. I could not
solidify the words. I trample

the long autumn. Beds of leaves glow
like fool's gold in sunlight. I want you
to linger as you once did—at the rim

of hearing; in the woman
brushing her white hair on a sidewalk;
in my own body's posture.
You were not so dead then.

You returned in a dream
to get clothes, I think. You didn't
know how to pack for your trip. Childlike,
you needed my help.

You were often horizontal, pieced together
like a leaf-quilt
from phone conversations.

You lay in a white bed, your voice
a brook inside your throat.

*

I can line up all the unkind things you said to me
like tools on hooks in the garage
with their blades for making
and unmaking.

And I can line up all my kindnesses.

And none of that can shovel over
the clean bones of failure:
the imperishable list
of what I did and did not do.

The Modulations of My Mother's Body

Her face is a sun I'm doomed
to orbit, her body a landscape I begin
to claim: the neck's V-shaped ingress,
its pillars of veins, the collarbone
a steep embankment, the throne
of shoulders, the slack folds gathering
and gathering along the arms
like sand drifts, the flattening
breasts, the abdomen's plateau, the soft
slope of buttocks, the gravel slide
of white thighs; how can I resist
the knees many-folded as roses, the veins
like raised roots, the feet blooming
blue, the stubby pebble toes,
the body that is ours,
the body contains me,
that hovers, angelic
at my edges.

Notes

p. 17) "Vacant Rooms at Hotel Infinity"
The title refers to "Hilbert's paradox of the Grand Hotel," a mathematical veridical paradox about infinite sets derived from the groundbreaking work of German mathematician Georg Cantor and presented by his colleague David Hilbert in 1924.

p. 53) "Bee Movies"
"And I, of ladies most deject and wretched
That sucked the honey of his music vows"

"Like sweet bells jangled out of tune . . ."

Ophelia in Shakespeare's *Hamlet*, act 3, scene 1

p. 54) "Bee Movies"
". . . for so work the honeybees
Creatures that by a rule in nature teach
The act of order to a peopled kingdom."

Canterbury in Shakespeare's *Henry V*, act 1, scene 2

p. 74) "Go West"
Translation of the italicized Italian:

What do you remember, old woman, of the Mediterranean?
The balconies, the red roofs like these?